East of the Cascades

Growing Up With Dad
East of the Cascades

A Mid-Century Memoir by
Cristy Quaale Carlson

ೞ

MP Methow Press

Twisp, Washington 98556

© 2023 Cristy Carlson

Published by Methow Press

P.O. Box 1213, Twisp, WA 98556
https://www.methowpress.com

Printed in the United States of America

ISBN 13: 978-1-7366537-6-0

For My Daughters, Penny & Melinda

.

Contents

CЗ ᘓ

One September day in 1947, a big yellow school bus picked me up at 7:30 am at the bottom of the hill to drive a dozen miles to the Madras Elementary School. It was miraculous, with indoor bathrooms and varnished wood floors. To me, the school seemed enormous, with a huge entrance at the top of many steps leading to my first-grade classroom.

School was so much fun because I could flush a toilet, drink water from a fountain, play with other kids, and make new friends. Before that, I had just one friend, Marilyn Horrigan, who lived at Cross Keys, about eight miles from our homestead. Marilyn and I had been baby buds since age one.

At school, stories were read to us. We learned to sight-read Dick and Jane books, memorize the alphabet, and count to 100. This was hard work, you know! So we had a special time to be quiet and rest on a blanket, lying on the floor.

Lunch came from home in a bucket with a thermos of milk. Recess was about running around, playing tag, being pushed in the swings, and riding the merry-go-round. School was out early for first and second graders. At 2:00, a private car picked Marilyn and I up to drive us home by 2:30.

So, why was I so excited to go to school?

HOME

I lived in a two-story homestead that was originally a stagecoach stop between Antelope and Sage Brush Springs. This frame house was built on a foundation of large rocks, with wadded newspapers stuffed in between the boards for insulation. The walls were papered on the inside. No electricity, no brothers and sisters, no running water. You could crawl underneath from one side to the other, if you were small.

Just before I turned 6 in August, I got my new twin bed, finally replacing my crib… which worked just fine all those years, until I could not stretch out as I was too tall. The front door was at the corner of the house that opened into to the living room, where the coal stove located in the middle was our only heating. That meant we had to open the bedroom door in the evening to warm up the bedroom, but I still needed a hot water bottle to warm my bed. This big downstairs bedroom was petitioned to separate Dad's bed and closet from my half. A curtain hung over the closet door, and the bedroom door was opened to let light in until I went to sleep.

The kitchen had a wood cook stove with a warming oven on top for cooking food, and it heated the kitchen and the little side room for the porcelain bathtub and shelving to hold the shaving gear and towels.

Bath water was a bit of a chore. We boiled water on the stove and added buckets of water pumped up from the cistern to make at least four inches of water. I was the first on the list to bathe, and the water was re-used by adding more hot water for everyone else to bathe.

We ate breakfast in the kitchen, and dinner and supper at the dining room. There was another room for a gas-operated refrigerator that kept foodstuffs chilled, and shelving for the canned goods. A partial wall was screened in with a wire netting to keep out the mice and bugs.

There was a big cold storeroom off the kitchen to house all the other stuff. It was really scary to open the door by myself, as once I saw a slaughtered hog hanging from a hook, and also a big salmon that was sold to us by the Celilo Falls Indians.

There were three very steep flights of stairs to climb before you opened a door to climb more steps leading up to the upstairs two bedrooms. My uncles Joe and Al slept on one side, and when my Aunt Mabel was home, the other one was her bedroom. Very, very cold rooms, or very, very hot rooms in the summer. But I had a dog, and a loving father!

About that dog. My loving father was not too happy when my Godmother showed up at the back door when I turned 5 years old, with a Cocker Spaniel puppy in tow. Dad did not think it was a good idea, possibly due to the responsibility that comes with a pet, but I held the puppy in my arms and pleaded. "Please! Please!" His heart melted, and it worked!

Dad helped me with naming my puppy, as I had no idea how to dream up a name. I was told it had to have a distinct sound so the dog would quickly recognize her name and come when called. Dad gave me a list of names to choose from, and "Trixie" was my pick. Dad agreed.

Trixie was a house dog in the daytime and slept on the porch at night in a special dog box piled high with rags, and on a few occasions when the thermometer would slip below zero, she was allowed to sleep inside by the kitchen in her daytime box.

So now you know why I was so excited to start school just to play with kids for five days in a row, learn to read and write, and have story time!

GRANDPARENTS

My Grandpa and Grandma Hyde would drive from Astoria to visit. Grandpa was a doctor and Grandma sewed clothes for me. They were very English and always wore nice clothes and drove a nice car. I remember some comments of disgust about why we would live in this old house on a dirt road with no electricity or bathroom. I also could not go bare-footed in the hot summer until Grandma went home. I don't think they ever spent the night with us!

I imagine they must have driven six miles to Lyle Gap and sleep at the Kennedy house, where my Godmother Eleanor, my Grandma's good friend, lived.

I do remember getting new clothes every time Grandma came along, with new hats and gloves for church. Grandma also taught me to say the Lord's Prayer and gave me a little framed Bible verse on a blue background to hang above my bed.

Grandpa Dr. Hyde once pulled my tooth when all I was going to do was show him how loose it was. He was holding my tooth in his big hand and the blood was dripping onto to my shirt making me a bloody mess. I jumped down and ran outside screaming and crawled under the fence so he couldn't catch me. He later died of a heart attack, when I was 8.

My Grandpa Quaale died before I was born. I was told he was working in Madras and was found dead in his car from a heart attack. Grandma Quaale had six children: Emil, Oswald (my dad), Alvin, Joseph, Ester, and Mabel. Ester died from bad well water when she was 11, and she had been my father's favorite sister. Grandma Quaale learned English as her second language from her kids going to school. Dad spoke Norwegian until he attended school in the first grade. Grandpa Quaale was about twenty years older than Grandma.

RANCH LIFE

Our closest town was the farming community of Gateway, which had a train depot, a country store, and a few houses. I was excited when we had to wait for the train to pass so I could count the hobos in the empty cars, and learn the different kinds of cars.

Noah's store was stocked with goods that farmers might need, besides groceries, and could also trade our eggs in for money or for goods. Noah, the storekeeper, was an older man and very kind. I loved to watch him slice the cheese stored on the counter under glass where he would wheel the cutter around. Our flour came in huge sacks that made the best dish towels, and sugar and other staples were in bulk. I sometimes was treated with a piece of hard candy.

This little store had everything, and even a gas pump where you pumped five gallons of gasoline up into a glass container where it was released by a hose to the car, and sometimes I was allowed to pump the handle back and forth.

Now, I lived on a ranch—so our meat was home-grown. We picked the oldest, toughest cows to slaughter, chopped the heads off chickens that no longer laid eggs, and butchered fat pigs. Successful deer hunting was also another meat source, and the venison was usually canned. I would sit at the table and chew and chew, sliding what I could not swallow under the table into Trixie's mouth. Very discreet! I am not sure if Dad ever knew.

On the other hand, I had fresh baked bread, cookies, pies, and cakes. Breakfast was eggs, bacon, fruit, and toast or mush. Dinner was a full-course meal with meat, canned vegetables from our garden, and potatoes. Plus dessert. Supper was another full-course meal with more meat and potatoes and dessert. This was all meant to feed the men so they could work hard all day. My favorite meal was simply mashed potatoes and gravy, and meat if I could chew it, and of course dessert and milk. I was very careful not to have any food touch that was on my plate. All food needed to be separated to eat it.

Milk came from our cow, so we churned butter, made buttermilk, and clabbered milk. The small gas-powered refrigeration unit was just large enough to store all the milk and the meat from the lockers and a few other things that needed to be kept cold.

What do I mean by "the lockers"? The old cows would be hauled off to the Van Wert Meat Lockers where Mr. Van Wert would butcher, slice, and grind up the meat for steaks, roasts, and a fair amount of hamburger to put in our locker drawer. Once a week we would visit the locker and pull out what we were going to eat the next week.

The chicken got put on the chopping block for a Sunday dinner. No need to freeze the chickens!

MOTHER

Let's go back prior to World War II, in the summer of 1941. My mother, Elizabeth Marie Hyde (nicknamed "Betty"), taught all eight grades in a one-room school at Lyle Gap, and was paid $75.00 a month, plus an extra $5.00 a month to be the janitor. My mother met my dad because she was teaching Uncle Emil's adopted son Leroy.

Mom's friend Jewel Clowers recalled how excited they both were to be expecting babies, both of them lying across her bed dreaming about whether the babies would be girls or boys, and what life would be like taking care of children.

A trip to the Bend Memorial Hospital, about sixty miles from the ranch, was made at the end of July when it was very evident my mother was in labor. That labor continued for three days and (according to Grandma Hyde) my Godfather, Bishop Bolster from Bend, went out into the streets to find volunteers for a blood transfusion. It was obvious that due to loss of blood and exhaustion a decision had to be made to perform a "C-section" to save one or both of us. My mother's last words were, "Whatever happens, it will be okay," and she passed away about two hours later.

So why did this happen? My Mother's regular doctor was on vacation and an older doctor took his place and the story told was that his mindset was "to let nature takes its course." But after three days of hard labor, it was realized that both of us were not going to make it as I weighed seven-plus pounds and was too large for the birth canal in her petite body of 5' 2".

The shock of all this came at the highest level of heat in the summer on August 2nd, but I was in good hands for seventeen days at the hospital until it was time I had to be released. My father was paralyzed about knowing what to do with a baby, and in the middle of wheat harvest! He was caught because he needed to work to make money that would support the family.

My Aunt Ruby and Uncle Emil, Dad's brother, stepped in to help and took good care of me and they grew very fond of me until things eventually had to change. Sometime in there I was christened by my Godfather, Bishop Bolster, and Eleanor Kennedy became my Godmother. As I look back, Aunt Ruby was an angel in my life as she was there looking after me in many ways until I was eventually moved home to be with Dad.

As the story goes, I was a real "going concern," playful and on the run, and grew on Ruby and Emil's hearts. They approached Dad to let him know they wanted to adopt me, as they could no longer just take care of me. Dad did not know what to do, but when he came to visit me around age 2, I ran to him holding my arms out, calling out, "Dad-dee, Dad-dee!" and that was it! Decision made!

So Dad came up with a plan to care for me. For the first few years, during the war, Grandma Quaale and Aunt Mabel helped to care for me and keep the house. Grandma lived in her own house and Mabel stayed at our homestead. Mabel went to work in Portland a couple of times, but said that wasn't for her, to "work away," so I believe that she took care of me most of the time, with a housekeeper hired once or twice until I was in about the sixth grade. Then I was on my own for a while along with Grandma's help from a distance.

I was a gregarious child in the early years, though, petting every dog and cat and sprawling across old Shep, our cow dog and original family pet. That was not always a good experience as he once bit me on the arm, drawing blood. I ran screaming to the house where I got all doctored up with red stuff and big bandages to go and play again. I guess I had to have a hot-day incident to understand what "Dog Days" meant! That did not stop me from petting strange dogs whenever we went to town to stroll on the board sidewalks. That meant I had to wear a harness when I got out of the car in Madras, until I was about 3 years old!

AFTER THE WAR

The war was over in 1945, and news came that I had an uncle coming home from the war on the Trailways bus. I was so excited to see him, and remember my Aunt Mabel and Grandma driving the car to the mailbox to wait for Joe. Can you imagine a good-looking man in an Army uniform getting off with his duffle bags? This was my first time seeing someone in uniform, and that was so different from farm overalls. I remember I was talking and asking questions a mile a minute—keeping to my nature—and it was so exciting. Arriving home, I wanted to show him our house and where he was going to sleep, that way up the steep, steep stairs to his bed that he would share with my uncle Al.

We were only a quarter mile from Highway 97, making it possible for people to stop to ask for food or gas.

One day I was out playing by the windmill that was pumping water into our cistern when a dark car drove into the driveway, and I was very anxious to see who might be coming to see us. A very tall black man—the first black person I had ever seen— got out of the car and wanted to know about getting some gas… and before I knew it, my Aunt Mabel and Grandma told me to get in the house, and I knew by the tone of their voice I was not where I was supposed to be. I think I was still a thumb-sucker around this time, so the cure was iodine painted on my thumb.

It was thought that I still needed an afternoon nap. No, I did not need a nap, but I was given no choice. Crawling out of my crib, I wrapped up in the lace-like window curtains to make a wedding dress like the one in the catalogs… yep, I got caught.

Speaking of catalogs, do you know what happened to them? The old ones went to the outhouse for our toilet paper, and the glossy pages were the last to be used!

When I was about 5, I started noticing that I was the only one with just a dad—no mother.

When I asked, "Where is my mother?" to my aunt or grandmother, their answer was that she was in Heaven.

So, my next question was "Where is Heaven?" The answer was that it was way up high in the sky. I would go outside and look to see if I could see her in between the clouds or in the clouds. Then when I was about 6 or 7, Dad took me to the cemetery on Memorial Day to put flowers on Mother's grave. At that time there were no caretakers, so Dad would bring a hoe to remove the weeds and a shovel to mound the dirt to give it a fresh look. A Mason jar was filled with water for the flowers to be placed at the headstone. When he was finished, he would say, "I guess that is all we can do," with tears rolling down his cheeks, making me also cry.

When I was about age 10, Dad began to treat me to a movie at the local theatre. This went on for the next seven years, and until I was married so I looked forward to seeing the movie to replace the sad Memorial Day cemetery emotions.

Another eventful moment at age 5! My tonsils had to go! Back to the Bend Memorial Hospital for a couple of nights and the day when I first tasted ice cream. I remember waking up with a really bad sore throat and ate an ice cream breakfast, and then wheeled into the men's ward for talking entertainment… or maybe that was my test to go home! Now all I wanted to eat was ice cream.

Getting dressed was no easy chore in the wintertime as I had to wear a garter belt. My first one had a harness with long garters that snapped to the long brown stockings, and later came the little garter belt I could put on myself to go to school. I was the only one that had to wear that thing, until I was in the third grade. I think somewhere around the second grade I started to unsnap my garters on the bus while I was still the only one on it, hurriedly rolling down a long stocking into one giant thick anklet sock. At least my legs were then bare, like all the other girls.

Elizabeth Marie Hyde (Betty Quaale)

Baby buds, Me and Marilyn Horrigan

Grandpa and Grandma Quaale, Dad standing, & little Al

Grandma Hyde, Me, and Shoes

Grandpa Hyde and Baby Me

Saluting the flag at Lyle Gap School, from left, Jim Matthews, Keith Farrell, Leroy Quaale, and teacher Betty Quaale.

Me at Nine Months

With Cousin Leroy

With Aunt Ruby

"Dad-dee! Dad-dee!"

A Little Bit of Greenery

Drawing in the Dirt, and the Old Barn

Sporting a Hat at Grandma Quaale's

Studio Photo at Age 2

When Dad Came to Bring Me Home for Good

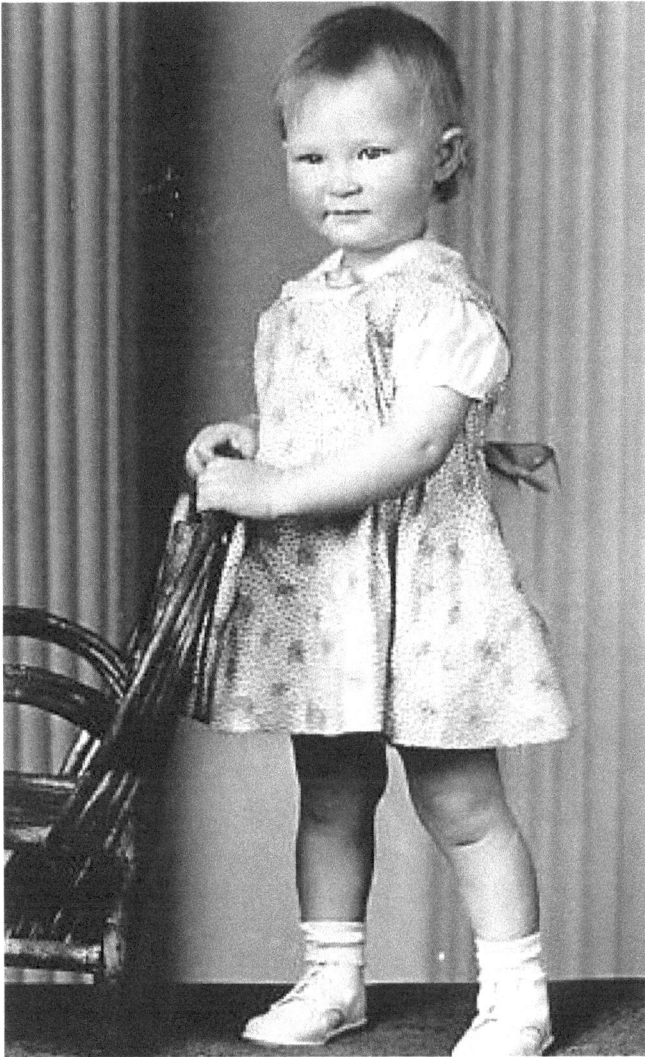

Another Pose from the Studio: Dad-dee's Girl

With Uncle Joe at His Homecoming

With Shep

With Mabel, Al, Grandma, Joe, Emil, and Dad

Studio Pose at Age 3

Summertime was just the best! I had an old tricycle with wide wheels that would go anywhere, and I had complete freedom with my puppy dog Trixie. I also had a new red wagon (a Christmas present) at about age 6. The dirt was my friend as I loved to carve out roads and build mountains with wood blocks. I had a great imagination and was going to find treasures, maybe find China. Among my favorite books were *Ali Baba and the Forty Thieves* and *The Three Billy Goats Gruff*, but *Peter Rabbit* was at the top of the list.

What was not on the top of my list was Dad's razor strap that hung over the tub in that little room. That was my visible reminder that I had to be nice, or else.

We had this housekeeper that came to work with her 4-year-old boy, and I don't remember much about him except: One day we were outside playing in the dirt and he had to pee, so I said, "Just pee behind this shed," and I was there to encourage him to see how high he could go on the wall… when his mother found us. That was not good! That night the razor strap came out—it was the first and the last time—as I cried before Dad hit my behind. But I got a whipping anyway.

"Jesus loves me this I know, because the Bible tells me so" was my favorite song that I learned going to Vacation Bible School every summer in Madras. I think my Godmother saw to it that I had a ride into Madras as Dad was really busy with working on the ranch and farm. I loved the stories of Noah and the Ark, David and Goliath, Abraham, and Moses that were read to me before I could read for myself.

Dad had a big wooden rocking chair with arms that was roomy for both of us where he would read to me. Once in a while I would beat on his newspaper to get his attention because I wanted to talk.

Now, can you imagine, three men smoking up a storm cloud that settled about four feet off the floor and me sitting in my little red chair and not have it bother me? The coal stove was converted into a wood stove where I set up my play area by the warm chimney. My uncle Albert, in Astoria, had built a stool for me and painted it white. When stood on end, and paired with my red chair, it looked kind of like Dad's desk! I spent hours and hours using the discarded envelopes and old mail dug out of Dad's wastepaper basket to write letters and "pay bills," to be like Dad. And I wrote a lot, even before I knew how to write.

DAILY LIFE

Our household was a bit unusual as I had two uncles and a grandmother living with us, and Aunt Mabel would come and go as would the housekeepers.

Harvest time meant hiring men to help with the dry-land wheat harvest for about two to three weeks in August. I was never afraid of these hired hands and would talk a leg off of them. Then one day, one of them asked me if I wanted to see him take his eye out to wash it. Of course, I said yes as I did not believe you could take your eye out. He did and it almost made me sick to my stomach as I thought it was a real eye.

Washing clothes was a Monday chore: On our little back porch that walked out to the cistern and windmill sat a washboard in a big tub and another tub to rinse. Big kettles were put on the wood stove to heat the water to make the wash water; I am not sure what happened with the rinse. But can you imagine what it was like to heat up the wood stove to make the hot water on a 100-degree August day? That took all day, and the clean clothes hung on the line until they were dry. It was freeze-dried time in the winter, along with an indoor laundry rack.

Tuesday was assigned to ironing: Dresses, shirts, pants, pillowcases, and even the sheets were ironed, taking most of the day to heat the irons on the wood stove then clamping on the handle. This went on until I was 8 years old, in 1949. Then we got an electric wringer-washer machine that sat on the back porch, and the iron came later as there had to be money to pay for the electrical panel, wiring, switches, and light bulbs in the middle of every room.

Wednesday and Thursday were driving somewhere: Visiting or making the ten-mile trip into Madras to pick up meat at the meat lockers, and staples that we could not buy in Gateway. Baking bread was ongoing along with pies and cookies, as was frying meat and roasting meat from our old cows on the range. Our eggs were fresh, the vegetables and fruits were canned— unless they were fresh from the garden. Roasted chicken continued to be a special treat on Sunday.

Friday and Saturday were more work days… but Sunday was a rest day: We attended the Cross Keys Church where my Dad would sometimes fall asleep and I would have to jab him to pop his head up. My Godfather delivered sermons, and this is where I learned about the Holy Ghost. I think I got mixed up about who the "Holy Ghost" was, comparing the stories about the "Boogie Man" and the ghosts on Halloween. I had a runaway imagination at night (as I was afraid of the dark) and just knew I had a ghost in my closet, so Dad would have to physically look in my closet and under the bed to give me the OK that I had no ghosts in my bedroom.

Winter days were short, cold, and dark days. Our house was very dark as we waited to light the kerosene lamps. New wicks were lit by a match and high flames were a bit frightening before adjustment was made, and the smell was not the best.

That was my reading light until sometime in my third year of school, when we got the electricity. Our windows would coat up with thick ice on the inside sometimes, and during big storms drifts of snow would show up inside near the front door. This was a drafty house! And now you know why I played by the chimney, and made up songs on the black upright piano until I was told "that was enough."

One Christmas Eve, Uncle Joe was chopping wood when he came back into the house with a badly bleeding thumb that made me almost faint as I could not stand the sight of blood. The axe had made a huge cut into his hand so immediate attention was needed. Our Christmas got delayed a bit as they hauled him off to the doctor in Madras.

CHANGES

The summer before I entered the second grade I got to take swimming lessons at the Redmond city pool. I loved water, but not this cold water, and the teacher wanted me to put my head under. Are you kidding me? That was not my idea of swimming. Guess what? I did not pass the test and I came home with no panties under my dress.

I knew where there was warm water because one time I got to go with my Sunday school class to the Ka-nee-ta where the pool was fed by the hot water from the springs. This pool had finished concrete-like sides but some of the bottom was still hard rock and someone told me they saw a snake in the pool. A new pool was built later on with a diving board, and I took every chance to go swimming as I loved the water, and really got serious about swimming around the eighth grade.

Speaking of water: In 1948, there was great flooding in the Pacific Northwest. Somehow, it happened at the exact time that

Dad was scheduled to take a truck loaded with cattle to sell to the Portland Auction yard.

First was the long haul up Cow Canyon, about fifteen miles from our ranch... on a scary, narrow, windy paved highway that resulted in many truck accidents because the brakes would heat up and quit working, killing many drivers and cows. So that was a bit scary to know when making my first trip winding around the curves and looking over into the canyon edge as there were no guardrails yet. I was going to see a big city and I was on an adventure. It took all day to drive that truck of steers over the plateau and down the Maupin Valley to the Columbia River Gorge and drive along the river to Portland.

That was when I really got scared, seeing houses and cars floating in the Columbia River from the flooding. It was a sight that was new to Dad, too, but he knew how to calm me down, feed me dinner, and get a warm room to sleep to be ready for the long drive to get home.

In the second grade I also had my eyes tested, and was I ever lucky because we discovered I could not see at a distance. Near-sightedness and astigmatism correction needed! No wonder I could not see the deer and coyotes pointed out to me in the hills way beyond.

Dad had just had his eye exam to get an "OK" to fly a plane. That's right! The next thing I knew, here comes Dad landing a yellow Piper Cub, and I'm wearing glasses. Somehow, Dad and my two uncles (the three were called the "Quaale Bros.") had smoothed a runway for the plane to land and added a hangar to the cow barn.

Oh, my goodness was I ever excited when Dad finally agreed to take me up in the plane! I did not know anyone else that had a dad that flew an airplane, and that was really important... as

I still had to use an outhouse. Wings, but no plumbing!

Later, I learned that Dad had wanted to go to war so he could fly airplanes, and was a bit jealous of Uncle Joe getting to go to war while leaving my dad and uncle on the farm to produce food. This irked Dad, as he had grown up very adventurous, riding a Harley with a sidecar to the Warm Springs Reservation to make $3.00 a day after his own dad had passed away and he had to become man of the household. He managed to create resources and was like an engineer, building a better future for his family. There wasn't anything he couldn't do, and he was definitely in charge.

My mother must have taught him a lot about love as I felt cared for. I was taught right from wrong, and as long I was doing what was right I had a license to go for it. As I was growing up, I did not realize how Dad suffered the loss of my mother and sacrificed his life to fulfill my needs. Dad let me know he was a one-woman man.

My friend Marilyn was sent to The Dalles where she was boarded to attend a private school before we entered the third grade. But I got to spend a few nights at her house before she left.

I was pounding on the piano making up songs until one day it became obvious that I should have piano lessons. Finding a piano teacher in Madras must have been a challenge, but somehow Dad found one within walking distance from the school, close to the housing project where dogs barked. I really liked learning and took lessons for about a year until my teacher made the point that I had to bend my fingers at a right angle. I thought I played best with flattened fingers, so she would whack my knuckles with a stick. I let Dad know that I did not need any more piano lessons from her. He was probably relieved!

This was indeed a time of change: Eyeglasses so I could see! My Dad had his yellow Piper Cub plane to take me flying so I could see the top side of the cows, trees, buildings, and the rim on the ranch! I loved being high up in the air. We had electricity! Plus a Schwinn bike for my eighth birthday, one that had a built-in button to blow the horn, handle bar grips, and a carrying rack basket behind my seat. That absolutely made my summer: learning to ride my bike, climbing the big elm tree, and playing on the swing to keep cool.

My Uncle Emil and Aunt Ruby had adopted an Indian baby from a down-south reservation, a boy about four years younger than me. His name was Larry and I adored his tanned-looking skin. Our fun was playing outside with animals and the dirt.

My Grandpa Hyde had heart failure in Astoria so my whole family drove forever to get to Astoria. While Dad and family attended the funeral, I was left with some unknown man in a white chef hat, and he was cooking my breakfast. I was not asked how I liked my eggs, and guess what? The plate of eggs was barely warm and the whites were really runny. It took me forever as I very politely forked them down with my toast. To this day, my eggs are cooked very hard. No jiggles!

One more item and it is a big one. We started getting water from the irrigation project, and each person could cultivate 160 acres. Our allotment was 640 acres for my family. Our land in the valley was transformed from sand dunes as high as fenceposts by moving the dirt around to fill in low spots. Dad must have rented or bought an earthmover that he pulled with his big Cat. Of course, I wanted to be included: Holding the long stick still was my job for Dad to shoot elevations using his new transit. It meant a lot to me as I could go to work like Dad.

Digging the ditches took another piece of equipment and somehow it all worked out to dam up the water by spreading a canvas across the ditch and then suck the water through a siphon tube to lay over the ditch that directed the water to each corrugated row. Clover was the first crop. White clover and red clover seeds must have been a great crop as new machinery started appearing on our place, and a little newer car to drive to Madras. The best part for me was Dad was happy as he did not have to worry if it was going rain. It was now all about planning when the water was going to come down the ditch to irrigate.

Now, 640 acres was too much to farm along with the cows and dryland wheat, so little houses were fixed up to attract renters. The Samson family had three pre-school boys, another was a man that had a mail-order bride from Europe, and another was just a bachelor. And then the really big house had a family of four, which had two boys younger than me. This was the house where games were introduced into my family, as we were invited down to play cards and have dessert.

SCHOOL DAYS

I loved school, and playing with all the kids. Mrs. Rawson was my third grade teacher, and that year held full days of school, including recesses. I jumped on the big yellow bus at 7:30 am and jumped off around 4 pm. Our school had expanded from eight rooms to about twenty by adding two more wings and a gym. I loved recess to play with other kids on the merry-go-round, the monkey bars, and swings.

Karen Lewis, still my dear friend today, and another new girl were always dressed in the prettiest dresses and both very smart in class. But they didn't play on the playground as they just walked around so as not to get messed up or dirty. I nicknamed them "Goody Two Shoes" and secretly wanted to be like them as they were smart, and I wanted to be a good reader, too. In the first grade I was taught sight-reading, as that was the current way of teaching, but now I had to learn phonics. I was not in the "Blue Bird" reading group, but worked hard to be with them. With Dad's help I got better, but I still had difficulties.

Then one day we had a blackboard game to see who the best at times-tables was. I was challenged by the smartest boy in class—Jim Blair, a tall red-haired freckled boy. I knew he was very smart, with numbers but with determination (and Dad's coaching!) I was going to beat Jim as it was so important for me to finish first.

And I WON!!! That moment gave me confidence that I could be at the top of the class.

I probably did not share with Dad how much he helped me become the winner of the blackboard competition. Looking back I now see how much encouragement and freedom I got from Dad, along with his hated lectures. (More about that later.) I went on to excel in arithmetic problems but disliked the story problems because I had to understand the story. Dad again was able to relate how to slice and dice the story part with common sense to figure out the actual math problem to get the answer.

One cold winter snowy day I decided after lunch that I would stay inside the classroom. Mrs. Rawson had playground duty, so I got the idea that I had to stay inside to protect the Bible that was on her corner of her desk, making everyone else go outside—including the "Goody Two Shoes." Well, someone snitched on me! Mrs. Rawson grabbed her paddle and took me down the hall where I admitted to the crime. Then I got a whack (it did not hurt), but I screamed and got one more whack until she stopped.

We had special days where you could bring your younger brothers or sisters to school. Steve Binder brought his little brother and he wet his pants making a puddle five or six feet long that ran past my desk. I saw it first and made a comment, so poor, embarrassed Steve had to get the mop and bucket and take the next half hour to clean up.

Another embarrassing moment was hearing Junior Wilson say the word "pregnant," and I asked very innocently what it meant. He made fun of me because I did not know the meaning, and in the future that just put me on notice to pretend I knew a new word, and then go look it up. Actually, I was a little intimidated to use Mother's ten-inch-thick dictionary she used when she had taught school, so I preferred to just ask Dad.

Friday afternoons were the best as we had "Music Hour." A teacher would read us a story, or a record was spun on the player to hear music. Just before Christmas vacation, Mrs. Rawson read us a story about Santa Claus… and guess what? That is when I found out there was no Santa!

CHRISTMAS

I was really sad and embarrassed because I truly believed Santa got my letter the year before since he brought the sled I wanted! I believe I was the only child that still believed in Santa Claus, but I was not going to let anyone know. There was no way I was going to tell my dad that I knew the truth, so every Christmas Eve the cookies and milk were laid out by his big rocking chair, and every year Santa ate the cookies, until I was about 12.

Counting down the days until Christmas Eve seemed to take forever. My Grandma would make lefse (Norwegian flat bread), and it was a big treat with lots of butter, sugar, and cinnamon rolled up tight. The tree was decorated with ancient paper ornaments, plus the homemade popcorn ropes that I got to help string. Grandma would sing "Silent Night" in Norwegian and English and then we could open our presents that were given to us from family and friends. I usually got hand-knitted mittens, long underwear, and very often doll clothes made by Ruby and Grandma Hyde.

Then it was time to prepare a plate of cookies for Santa and carrots for the reindeer, line up our chairs to display our socks so Santa knew who we were, and then I was off to bed. I would try my best to stay awake to catch Santa, and once I thought I heard the reindeer on the roof.

One year I asked Santa for a baton. I not only got a baton, but I got the most expensive one... extra-long with the brilliant sparkles. Santa always seemed to know what toys or dolls I liked. There were the big toys, the leather-looking doll buggy with a sun visor to shade my dolls, the best sled, and the bright red wagon that hooked to my tricycle. Those were among my favorites.

ALONG WITH DAD

During the slow time of the year, Dad took me wherever he went—visits to town offices that had pot belly stoves to warm up business meetings, picking up parts needed to repair equipment, and many trips to the auction yard where he would raise his hand to bid and purchase bulls and heifers.

One time we hauled home a one-ton Herford bull to add to the growing cattle herd. We had Hereford cows (the white-faced ones!) and, oh, how fun to ride along with Dad and uncles in the little Jeep to feed them. One section of the road had the biggest mud puddle, and I loved to see how high the water would spray when driving through. *Loved* it… but sometimes we would get stuck in the mud and everyone got out pushing—except me and the driver.

The cows were wild, but you could not tell me that I couldn't go pet a newborn calf. Dad never stopped me from trying even though there was no chance, and he was right! He was very smart to allow me to experience my failures instead of telling me I couldn't do a particular thing.

Winters were harsh, having to drive about two miles on a daily basis in all weather conditions to get up where the cattle were pastured during the winter. Water troughs were layered with ice, and hay was put out sprinkled with molasses, but for me it was exciting stuff and the best part was stopping off at Grandma's house for coffee and cookies. Hot chocolate for me, though!

I was allowed to be on the scene for de-horning the cows. Hands would clamp off the cows' horns, squirting blood everywhere, and curious me got too close only one time.

Branding was another hurtful sight, and so was punching the ears for tagging. Once was enough to watch the castrating of a calf to make a steer. Vaccinating was tolerable!

Summertime was also alone-time, with no kids near to play with. With my new high-powered bike, I rode one mile up and over the hills to Grandma's house for cookies and Kool-Aid.

My Dad told the story about how a famous family had two kids kidnapped and held for ransom. This was to put me on notice to be aware of highway traffic as a car could slow down and open up the trunk and put me in. So I made a plan. Get way back in the brush, watch up and down until no cars were coming and then make a running start to go as fast as I could to peddle over the highway, gaining as much speed as possible to be out of sight before a car would go by.

I was also told to watch for snakes. If one was in the road, I would stop and size up the situation on how to get around it. My best plan was to gain enough speed, and just as my wheels ran over the snake I would jam on my brakes… but never on a coiled up snake (most likely a rattler), only bull snakes or garden snakes.

Another thrill was to ride on the wheat-threshing combine. Dad would drive the Cat to pull the machine, and my uncle Joe was the best hand to sew the top of the wheat sacks shut, laying them down in a chute, making a place for me to sit on top before he pulled the cord that dropped the sacks to the ground.

What a thrill to be dumped in the field! I was also taught how to make gum by threshing the wheat in my hand and chewing to make cud or gum.

Summer was also time to play with my dog and dolls. Of course, Trixie was obedient and rode in the doll buggy all wrapped in blankets along with my dolls.

But I did have one thrilling experience taking a bus all the way to Astoria. Somehow it was safe to put me on a bus in Madras that made it all the way with one transfer in Portland, with someone making sure I got on the correct bus. I wonder who!

Astoria was a cold, damp, rainy city as the warmest was in the 70s, and I liked summer sunshine with temperatures in the 80s or 90s. Grandma Hyde had a little apartment with all her stuff everywhere. Lace doilies, rugs, crystal, and china—so different from our farm furnishings.

I was entertained with learning her sewing skills and was very happy to spend hours and hours learning how to crochet, and walking up and down the hills. We were picked up one time so she could babysit a ship-captain's child, and they had the most beautiful house I had ever seen. Indescribable!

Then Dad came to take me home.

Wow, what a surprise he had for me as he took me to Janzen Beach to ride a rollercoaster for the first time. I was so excited to watch the train of seats being pulled to the top, and then hear the screams as it raced around the track.

My wish came true to sit in the front seat, all buckled up to start the long pull uphill. I had no idea how high we were, but as we neared the top and started to fall down the track I was screaming along with the others. I was so little hanging onto the bar and Dad was full time in charge of keeping me grounded to the seat so that I never realized there was a danger. When it was time to get off, I asked if we could go again. I had never seen Dad so dizzy so was not surprised when his answer was a flat "NO," end of discussion!

Around 10 years old, my social life grew. My Aunt Ruby and Uncle Emil built a new house with a basement that was filled with games and a place to play with new cousins by marriage, Joey and Lenny. Joey, a girl, was one year older than me and went to the Seventh Day Adventist School. Lenny wanted to be a doctor and got a doctor's kit the previous Christmas, and Joey got a nurse's kit. They needed a patient. Since I did not have a profession all picked out, I was happy to be their patient.

I loved going to Ruby's. Joey's parents were also building a big house, but I spent the night with her while they were living in a machine shed with curtains to divide the beds. And then came their house that was so big it even had a dumbwaiter.

One summer I played with a white angora that I must have gotten at Easter. Grandma Hyde also rode the bus to come see me because she wanted to make sure I had a short-short haircut… and it did not make a difference that I wanted long hair. I also had to wear shoes again while she visited. Ugh! She wore those black clunky high heels and a big corset that went from top to bottom and had garters for her stockings. In the 90-degree heat! Such a contrast to my other Grandma, who had no corset and wore canvas shoes with cutouts to relieve her bunions.

FURTHER SCHOOLING

Yay!!! It was time to go back to school with new clothes from Sears Roebuck and Montgomery Ward. No matter how hot it was, I was going to wear my new sweater on the first day of school. I was very lucky to get Miss Rose, a beautiful lady with long dark hair, petite with red lipstick and high heels, for my teacher. This year was a first step toward becoming an upper-classman.

In January, we had the Gideons visit our room to talk about Jesus, and we were all invited to accept Christ as our Savior. I knew all about Jesus from church, where I kneeled to pray and stood to sing, so I accepted the invitation! I still have my copy of the New Testament inscribed with my name and dated January 12, 1951.

Moving forward to Mother's Day in May, we had an assignment to write a poem about our mother. Of course, I did not have one so thought I would just pretend and make up something. It was so hard because Dad was all I had, so I wrote down a couple of lines and went to the front of the room when it was my turn to read my poem. I started to read out loud and then broke down crying. Miss Rose came to my side and asked why I was crying as she did not realize I did not have a mother.

The next year, fifth grade, was really big as we got to leave our classroom and walk to the chorus and band room. I was shy about singing, but we had to sing to be placed in the choir. I was labeled a soprano. Baseball was added to our sports. If I could ever hit the ball, I could run fast enough to make it to first base, but not being much of a hitter I became one of the last kids picked to be on a team.

A new pink brick Episcopal Church was built a block over from the high school. We attended this church that had a residing reverend, an organ, wood pews, green kneeling pads, and a cross that held the hymn page numbers—usually four for each service. Later I learned that my Uncle Albert made that cross in memory of my mother. The basement served for Sunday school, bazaars, dinners, and other church activities. Dad was not big on social things, but I was—so we attended some events.

Grade six was my year to be a little bit rebellious, and I'm not sure why. Maybe it was an exercise to grow my personality as I certainly was not rebellious toward my Dad. His way of teaching "right from wrong" was to set me down square to his frame and look him in the eye as he lectured me, and I was expected to answer all his questions before I could get off the chair. Torture!

My first "man teacher" was Mr. Tabor, a little guy and not very tall. I guess I was practicing my rebellion as I one day decided to make fun of the poor man. I raised the hinged lid of my desk to tell my neighbor that Mr. Tabor should be called Mr. Robot (Tabor sort of spelled backwards) and was giggling when a voice appeared out of nowhere, "Is that so?" I was placed in a chair and put in the corner at the front of the room. That did make a mark that changed my behavior!!!

Sometime during this year, Aunt Mabel left to explore the

world and I was now responsible for taking care of myself. Well, I did not like to wash my face and brush my teeth at night, so I imagine I did not look the best for a couple of days.

Arithmetic was still my best subject… and I wanted a bra to wear so I could look grown up. I had an undershirt that had skinny straps and would try to show my straps so kids would think I was wearing a bra. So this was my entry into junior high life.

In March of 1953, I went with Grandma, Mabel, and Dad to Silverton to visit some really short people, Chris and Annie Hansen, to celebrate my dad's father's sister's 50th wedding anniversary. Chris Hansen was just five feet tall, smoked a pipe, and smelled like sharp cheese. Annie was about the same height.

I was delighted to meet two more teenaged girls. Alma was about my age and was fun to play with, and she knew where the cracked walnuts were stored in a pantry, walnuts which Annie had put up for the winter months. We ate at least one-half of a quart jar as they were the best and went down so easy because they were already shelled. After a while, we both were not feeling so good and were found out. What an embarrassing moment!

This was the year for me to go visit my English Grandma Hyde in Astoria for two whole weeks, a particularly fun visit as my Uncle Albert was then manager of the public pool, so I got to go play in the cool water and try to swim with my head out of the water. Aunt Ebba played bridge and introduced me how four ladies could sit at a card table to play cards all afternoon and then eat dessert. One evening I was taken to see a big sandy beach called Cannon Beach to watch the sunset. They had a playground area that had bumper cars, and I was thrilled when Uncle Albert asked if I wanted to drive a bumper car on my own. Of course, the answer was "YES" even though I had no idea how, but I was all-in for fun. I got bumped by lots of cars until I got so I could bump, too. This was my first time seeing an ocean beach, as Astoria was on the Columbia River and had a port for the ships to come in, but no sandy beach.

It was great to have other activities because Grandma had moved to a small apartment on a steep hill with a sidewalk. What I remember most was being given all her lace and fabric scraps from her sewing stash. Now, I had no patterns, but had a little doll that I could wrap the material around to cut to make a pattern and make a dress. I was pleased and happy to learn how to sew.

As I look back, Grandma Hyde was a very kind person and worked hard to keep in touch with my life and make sure I had nice clothes to wear, and learn about Jesus. There were only a few times that she shared anything about my mother, and I did not know what questions to ask.

Just before grade seven, I learned that I was special, as Grandma explained that I would have bleeding once a month within a year or so… so later on I could have babies. WHAT?

I did want four children, but I did not know I had to bleed every month to have babies. I was sent home with a pack of sanitary pads. Her story was that she did not know where babies came from until her doctor husband had to tell her about the "birds and the bees" on their wedding night. Well, I wasn't sure where they came from either!

Montgomery Ward and Sears and Roebuck catalogs (each about two inches thick) had pictures of everything you could possibly want and would arrive two times a year: winter and summer, with smaller ones in the offseason. They were called "wish books" as no money was spent unless it was a need.

When I got old enough to know about "comic books," I would pressure Dad to buy me one at the grocery store and I would pace my reading to one page per day so it would last until I got another one… and I saved them all to re-read again and again.

It was hard for me to read from our books on the bookshelf as the stories were beyond my understanding and not interesting to me.

Entering grade seven was a thrill, and I started noticing boys. Riding the school bus was an opportunity to sit next to Dave Stewart and after a few months he put his arm on the back of my seat. I just melted! We also had to dress down in shorts for PE and play sports in the gym or outside if it was good weather. Showers: now that was an interesting introduction, to see others naked and to compare bra sizes.

Around 4:00 pm I would come home from school through the back door looking for a cookie or something to tide me over to dinner time. The best deal was to steal globs of bread dough from the bottom of the loaf before it was baked… some loaves grew to be more like buns! My jobs for dinner: peel the potatoes with a knife, set the table, and help wash the dishes after. We had a big family of three hungry men, skinny me, one woman to cook, and my dog Trixie.

Around the age of 12 or 13, I tried out to be a cheerleader for the football team. I was chosen, and the next thing I knew, someone thought we should make our outfits… blue culottes. Everyone else had moms, so this project was up to me if it was to be. I had no sewing machine, so I set out to read the pattern, cut out the pieces, baste the seams… and then rode to grandma's house to use her treadle sewing machine, and after a fashion I had something that fit.

This was the beginning of many decades of sewing all my

clothes and all my children's clothes. Why? Because I could create my own fashions to make the clothes fit my tiny 21-inch waist.

I had some girl problems in the seventh grade. Girls can be so mean.

I thought I had some girlfriends, but they turned against me and ignored me during recess. They walked away from me on the school grounds, and talked behind my back giving me funny looks. This went on for at least three months, long enough to make me cry at night. Dad would ask me what was wrong.

This was a very lonely time. I would pretend it did not hurt during the day, and then cry at night. It was also my first year having the Warm Springs Indians in our school, and I tried to make friends. They were sort of nice, and then also turned mean. One of the girls, Janice, jabbed her lead pencil in my thigh above my knee, leaving a pencil-dot tattoo for the next ten to fifteen years.

Then, out of nowhere, here comes "Miss Goody Two Shoes." Karen.

Karen was my new friend! She lived on the Agency Plains and had to ride the bus a long way, too. Her parents originally moved from Eugene, Oregon, to buy some farmland with irrigation water. No one else comes to my mind as a friend that year because my friend Sharon had turned against me.

Three Feet Tall, Just Like the Squash!

At Age 5

Caught With My Stockings Rolled Down!

On Billy

At Center, Godmother Eleanor Kennedy

Me and the Old House

Aunt Mabel and Grandma Quaale

Uncle Al, Mr. Daniels, Dad, Uncle Joe… and Trixie!

New Clothes from Grandma Hyde

Dad's Piper Cub

The Hereford Herd

The Truck I Bounced Around In with Dad

Yes, That's My Wheat Sack Chute!

Lasting for over four decades, the Dipper was the source of many happy memories for millions of Amusement Park enthusiasts.

The world famous Big Dipper Roller Coaster was the main attraction.

Built in 1928 by the legendary Coaster Designer Carl Phare, the Big Dipper

In My Play Clothes at Age 11

Chris and Annie Hansen, at Left

At the Hansen 50th Anniversary Celebration

With Trixie by the Kitchen at the Old House

The Rabbit Hutch… and One Big Angora!

At Marilyn's House, in My Favorite Dress

At Our New House

A NEW HOME

What a change: A new four-bedroom house with redwood siding, green shingles on the roof, and a big mahogany front door. It had four huge windows about two feet from the floor, and hardwood floors. And a white electric stove and refrigerator, and a sink with a faucet for running hot and cold water. The blue bathroom was huge with built-in cabinets, a long counter with a sink, and a tile shower over the bathtub.

My first shower at home was a miracle. I drained the hot water tank, drawing Dad's attention to knock on the door. It was time to get out!

The house was beautiful, and the only thing that came from the old homestead was the oil central-heating stove that was bought shortly before we moved. There was a small wood burning stove in the new kitchen for heat. The kitchen was bright yellow with red and yellow linoleum, two-tone green walls for the big living room, and a blue bedroom for Dad.

I even got to choose the shade of pink I wanted for my bedroom! It came with sliding mahogany closet doors and two double-hung windows that overlooked the porch where Trixie's box sat under my window.

I believe it was springtime when we moved and I honestly cannot remember the move. I do recall that the big front porch (about 4' x 20') was a thick concrete pad. Now, someone had just given me clamp-on roller skates and I needed a place to practice, so you can imagine how excited I was to have a big flat surface to skate on... until Dad found me!

Oh, oh.... He almost cried as he showed me the indented marks that I had carved in the uncured concrete. I cried, too. I'm sure this was another moment of Dad giving me a lesson on thinking first before I do a thing… or something like that. As years went by, the dents were less noticeable, except for a puddle showing up where I made my turns when it rained a lot or the lawn sprinkler sprayed water on porch.

Someone who probably liked roller skating hooked up with the Grange Hall people to create a roller rink for kids of all ages to skate. I did not have to wear my clamp-on skates as they rented out real roller-skates. Dad was great to take me and hang around town until it was time to head home, and this was a place to have fun with the boys as they were getting to be more interesting.

Sometime that year Dad hired Myrtle from San Francisco and she came to live with us, bringing a TV, a sewing machine, and a big bedroom full of stuff. This was after a trial run of a couple of months.

Well, Myrtle was more than a housekeeper! She could milk the cow, plant a garden, take care of chickens, and had a barking Pomeranian. She taught me how to kill a chicken, scald the bird, pluck the feathers, and cut the chicken open to remove the guts. That part really made me vomit, so I wore a clothespin over my nose. My reward was that I learned the proper way to cut up the chicken.

My biggest dream was to become a teenager, and this was the summer! I would ride my bike to Grandma's house, and visit the men out in the fields to give them her cookies.

About chocolate chip cookies. I decided to make them all by myself somewhere around age 11. I was so proud of myself as Dad took a bite and said, "Very good." My uncle Al took a bite and quickly spit it out as it was too salty… Instead of ½ teaspoon I measured ½ cup! I noticed that Dad did not eat the entire cookie. I had to agree they were terrible.

I was taught how to recognize rattlesnakes as they were the ones that could kill you.

One day, on my outing to visit an abandoned house, I spotted a rattlesnake in my pathway to the front steps, so I decided to kill it. I gathered up a stack of rocks and started throwing the rocks until it stopped moving. I was so proud! I had to show my Dad when he came home from work.

Sage Brush Springs had long been a favorite place to gather watercress for salads and wade in the water, but after irrigation came in, runoff washed deep gullies, making the springs impossible to play in, and the watercress was no more.

I could also walk to "Old Maid Canyon" about a mile away to wade in some water. The story goes that there was a strong unmarried woman who built her homestead in the area, and I was told that she had "a religious background," whatever that was supposed to mean.

My white angora baby rabbit grew into a huge bunny that took forever to brush, so it usually had matted hair. I would take him out of the hutch to eat white clover while I trimmed back the matted hair. This would take me days and days to get it all done.

Trixie had long golden curly fur, so she was another project. Cheatgrass seeds buried in her ears that were the worst to pluck…and then I had to trim the fur between her toes to dig the cheatgrass buried in her skin. She was a real sight to see, all the patchwork of uncut hair making her a bit lop-sided, and I could sense her embarrassment.

AROUND THE RANCH

Strawberries were always there for the picking.

Climbing the huge elm tree got a little scary at times. Climbing over the corral to visit the horses one time, I plunged an iron spike into my inner thigh and blood was spurting while I ran to the house for help.

Horses! I wanted one of my own to ride. Dad finally caved in and found a horse somewhere. I named him "Whitey" because it was a very light-colored horse with some darker patches. I was half-way trained, but now I had to put the bridle on and the hike the saddle over the top. I did manage to pass the test and now had one more animal to care for. Dad made it easy on me, letting me use the pasture close to the house with water, the one we called the "South 40." Now I had more responsibilities, but this one was fun as I could ride Whitey everywhere instead of walking.

All the awesome plane rides I had with Dad continued to be highlights. I loved to take off and look down on everything. From our house we could see the Blue Mountains (also called the "Mutton Mountains") and I remember how shocked I was to find there were really green mountains with lots of trees.

One time, we were flying over the rim and Dad was explaining to me the updrafts and downdrafts in the air. He was going to show me what it felt like to be in a downdraft. We must have dropped about two hundred feet before we pulled up. What a rush!

I asked if he would go back and do it again. That was the wrong thing to say as I got another lesson for not understanding his example of how dangerous a downdraft could be.

We had lots of guns: shotguns, .22s, 30-06s, and rifles. I was taught not to mess with them, so I did not. But we had a ton of jackrabbits that would eat massive amounts of our dryland wheat in the summer. After dinner, we took off to shoot them, and it was fun to get five or six at a time... but I did not shoot cottontails.

Here I am, 13 years old, and I get all the instructions for the fifteenth time about making sure the gun is on safety at all times, except when you are going to pull the trigger. Finally it's my turn to shoot and Dad is driving. He spots a jackrabbit, and stops so I can get out and take aim. Well, it took a bit for me to aim to make sure I was going to hit him, and the rabbit ran away. I get back in the car pointing the gun to the floorboard and it goes "BOOM." Dad just looked at me and said, "See what happens when you don't put it back on safety." His way of teaching me was giving me a permanent brain imprint on how to do it right.

THE END OF CHILDHOOD

One last year of grade school. Karen Lewis, whom I admired, had a mom who was the greatest, and the best cook. Karen also had a little brother, Rich. By the end of summer, I was also good friends with Sharon Piercy again. She had an older sister, and her parents owned both the downtown movie house and the drive-in. Her mom was the ticket taker in the window, and her dad ran the movie projector. Sharon's job was to usher and make popcorn and sell candy. These two moms treated me like another daughter and I claimed them as my new moms.

Riding the school bus became another social party, as it was fun to have a boy come sit by you. Several girls were starting to like boys, so I started noticing what boys liked and did not like.

I did not find much to pick from, so I quickly moved on to sewing. Dad would not care about the cost of the material I bought, because it was much cheaper to sew my clothes than buy them. Since Myrtle had moved in full time and was so nice about teaching me more about how to sew, I was free to use her sewing machine. I was amazed at how she could play the piano, so I also started to play more.

My grade 8 teacher was Mr. Keithly, the best teacher ever. He kept us interested in learning new subjects. His special interests were geology and our music programs.

The Christmas Concert was where I was in the choir, and Sharon played the clarinet. Karen had a great soprano voice and was chosen to sing for our graduation. Throughout the year, there were more PE comparisons in the locker-room while taking showers, and more competition to play on teams for volleyball, basketball, baseball, and so on.

This was also the year of first being asked to spend the night with a girlfriend. Karen was first to ask me, and I was thrilled to ride a different school bus.

My social life was beginning to look promising as I had the start of two great girlfriends and two moms. When I invited Karen to spend the night at our house, she was also delighted to get to ride my school bus and see where my house was, and she liked my pink bedroom with a double bed.

We had a mandatory dance class at school, meaning that we had to learn the waltz and move our feet together, learn how the boy holds the girl, and how the girl fits in the hold as the boy leads. Interesting and embarrassing at first, but I loved the idea! I soon learned I was pretty good at keeping the beat while only some of the boys got it. This went on for about six weeks to prepare us for the sock hops later on in high school.

Toward the end of the year we were bused to visit Madras Union High School, noting our next step to register for our freshman year.

Gee! Look! We would have our own combination lockers to stack our stuff, and get to have hall time to talk and walk between classes, and hot lunches in the cafeteria. Two classrooms were in an adjacent school building where the girls could take cooking and sewing classes and a shop room for the boys, but we wouldn't go there until we were sophomores.

That final Memorial Day of my childhood was easier, as the cemetery had hired caretakers. A dozen red roses and a mason jar of water were all we had to bring, before Dad and I went to see the movies. *Shane*, with Alan Ladd, was very sad, opening with a funeral scene. I cried!

The summer between grade eight and my Freshman year is a blur. Surely I rode Whitey, a lot, and picked strawberries, plucked chickens, and sewed clothes. My hair was short again, so I must have had a visit from Grandma Hyde... and worn shoes again.

Now the blur clears as Clark Mason, a neighbor boy, appears in my memory.

My first date!

Turning 14 on August 2nd and being asked out on a date to the drive-in movie was a big deal. Dad knew the boy, who lived about a mile from us, and was going to be a senior in high school, so he halfway agreed that I could go to the drive-in movie. I wore a dress with a short poodle jacket and did not enter the living room until Dad had let Clark in. Then I heard Dad say to Clark, "Well, so what are your intentions?" I think Clark (5'-8") just shrunk and found a voice to look up to (6'-2") Dad and answered, "I just want to take her to the movies."

Clark had an older model Buick with a hard top and a gear shift. We arrived at the drive-in at the entrance gate and parked somewhere with a good speaker. He asked me to scoot over next to him, and he put his arm around me. Wow!

I got a little warm but I was not going to take off my poodle jacket even when he started the car and turned on the heater. Yes, I got really warm, but my jacket was not coming off! I finally let him kiss me… and this kiss was not what I imagined from reading the romance magazines.

It was good to get over the scare of having that first date, but I did not need to have another one for a while.

I was on the verge of Happy Days!

Colophon

Growing Up With Dad East of the Cascades, by Cristy Quaale Carlson,

was set in Garamond by Methow Press.

The cover design is by Greg Wright.

The cover photo is from the Quaale archives.

Manufactured by LightningSource, LaVergne, Tennessee.

www.ingramcontent.com/pod-product-compliance
Lightning Source LLC
LaVergne TN
LVHW010318070426
835511LV00026B/3494